EDGE
BOOKS

Surprising Facts About Being an

ARMY SOLDIER

by Kristin J. Russo

Consultant:
Kurt Waeschle, Chief of Operations
Navy Region Northwest Fire and Emergency Services

CAPSTONE PRESS
a capstone imprint

Edge Books are published by Capstone Press,
1710 Roe Crest Drive, North Mankato, Minnesota 56003
www.mycapstone.com

Library of Congress Cataloging-in-Publication Data
Names: Russo, Kristin J., author.
Title: Surprising facts about being an Army soldier / by Kristin J. Russo.
Description: North Mankato, Minnesota : Capstone Press, [2018] | Series: Edge
  books. What you didn't know about the U.S. military life | Includes
  bibliographical references and index. | Audience: Grades 4-6. | Audience:
  Ages 8-14.
Identifiers: LCCN 2017008348| ISBN 9781515774297 (library binding) | ISBN
  9781515774334 (ebook pdf)
Subjects: LCSH: Soldiers--United States--Juvenile literature. | United
  States. Army--Juvenile literature.
Classification: LCC UA25 .R83 2018 | DDC 355.00973--dc23
LC record available at https://lccn.loc.gov/2017008348

Editorial Credits
Nikki Ramsay, editor; Sara Radka, designer; Laura Manthe, production specialist

Photo Credits
Getty Images: bennymarty, 18, Brendan Smialowski, 13, Chris Hondros, 7, 17, Gabriel Mistral, 21, Junko Kimura,
15, Paula Bronstein, 16, Scott Olson, 10; Newscom: Andrew Craft via ZUMA Wire, 5, JR Ancheta/ZUMAPRESS.
com, 29, KRT, 25, LCpl. John E. Lawson Jr./DOD/US DOD Photo/ZUMAPRESS.com, 14, Mark H. Milstein/
Red Dot/Red Dot/ZUMAPRESS.com, 24, Sgt. Michael J. Macleod/ZUMA Press, cover, Spc. Nikayla Shodeen/
Planet Pix via ZUMA Wire, 23, Ssgt. Vito T. Bryant/Planet Pix via ZUMA Wire, 9, Stacy L. Pearsall/DOD/Sipa
Press, 11; Shutterstock: AV_Studio, 19, Joseph Sohm, 8, Sumate Gulabutdee, 12; Wikimedia: U.S. Army/Sgt. Aaron
LeBlanc, 27

Graphic elements by Book Buddy Media.

Printed in the United States of America.
010364F17

TABLE OF CONTENTS

GO ARMY!

From 1775 to 1783, colonial militia fighters and full-time soldiers joined to fight the British in the American Revolutionary War. This force was the first army in the United States. Many of these soldiers had no gunpowder or equipment. Abigail Adams, who would become First Lady, even melted down her pewter dishes to make bullets.

To face the strong army of Great Britain, they had to use guerilla warfare. This means they didn't fight in a regular way. They planned secret attacks and took the British by surprise. It took eight years, but the Continental army finally beat Great Britain and won independence for the new United States.

Today there are more than 1 million soldiers serving in the reserves and on active duty in the U.S. Army. Many people know that the life of a soldier is hard. Training is difficult and they might serve in harsh conditions far from home. Yet people may be surprised to learn about the updated weapons and technology soldiers use in a new kind of warfare. They may also be surprised to learn about the variety of jobs in the Army. Some are artists, and some even fight bugs!

FACT Some colonial militia members were called "minutemen." This is because they always had their weapons and equipment with them so that they could be ready to fight quickly.

Soldiers train in mock battle exercises to ensure they are ready for combat.

Chapter 1

BECOMING AN ARMY SOLDIER

The U.S. Army has protected the United States for more than 200 years. Soldiers in the Army may travel to different parts of the world to work for peace and to fight. It takes a very special person to live the life of an Army soldier. Not everyone is cut out for this difficult job.

Enlist

Men and women who want to **enlist** in the Army should meet with a recruiter. A recruiter will answer very important questions about becoming a soldier. Enlistees should ask questions about what jobs in the Army they would be good at and enjoy. Recruiters will show them videos about training and a soldier's duties.

Physical Fitness

In order to join, men ages 17 to 21 must be able to do 35 push-ups and 47 sit-ups. They must be able to run 2 miles (3.2 kilometers) in less than 17 minutes. Women ages 17 to 21 must be able to do 13 push-ups and 47 sit-ups. They must be able to run 2 miles (3.2 km) in less than 20 minutes. The test is a little easier, but not much, for men and women ages 22 to 34.

Is the Army for Everyone?

There are reasons why a person would not be allowed in the Army. The Army will not accept anyone with a tattoo on their face or hands. Also, people who stretch their earlobes to wear special earrings are not eligible to apply.

Some medical problems, such as serious eye disorders or injuries, will keep someone from joining. However, wearing glasses is not a problem.

Army recruiters meet with civilians interested in joining the military to answer questions and conduct interviews.

 FACT **Recruits** who meet the guidelines can join with their friends. Up to five friends can enlist together, and they will be stationed together and allowed to work together. People who join through the Buddy Program are also eligible for extra bonus pay.

enlist—to voluntarily join a branch of the military

recruit—a person newly enlisted in the armed forces and not yet fully trained

WEST POINT MILITARY ACADEMY

Soldiers who attend the U.S. Military Academy at West Point become officers as soon as they graduate. More than 13,000 students apply to West Point every year. Only about 1,200 are accepted. Most students must have top grades and play a **varsity** sport to be considered. All students are asked, "Why do you want to attend West Point?" They should be ready for this question with a good answer.

High school juniors are invited to attend camp during the summer at West Point. The students live in the barracks, attend leadership workshops, and play sports. The camp is fun but challenging. Attending the camp helps students decide if they really want to apply to West Point.

"Cadet gray" has been worn by cadets at West Point since 1816, when the Secretary of War formally approved the uniforms for use.

The Cadet Pledge

All students at West Point are called cadets. Before their first year, all cadets must make a pledge that they will not "lie, cheat, or steal, or tolerate those who do." This pledge is based on West Point's honor code. If a cadet gets caught lying, cheating, or helping someone else lie or cheat, they could be **expelled**.

The Plebe Bible

First-year students at West Point are called "plebes." All plebes are told to read *Bugle Notes*, otherwise known as "The Plebe Bible," before they begin their freshman year. *Bugle Notes* has serious information in it, such as the cadet pledge and principles of leadership. It also includes fun facts, such as the names of West Point's past and present mascots — mules named Spartacus, Ranger, Trooper, and Traveller.

FACT Robert E. Lee, American Civil War general for the South, and Ulysses S. Grant, general for the North, both graduated from West Point. Grant's name was actually Hiram Ulysses Grant, but the congressman who nominated him to West Point made a mistake on the application. From then on, he was known as Ulysses S. Grant.

varsity—the principal team representing a high school or college in a sport or other competition

expel—to throw out or ban

Chapter 2

TRAINING

BASIC TRAINING

No one becomes an Army soldier overnight. It takes weeks and sometimes months of hard work and training for a new recruit to be ready for combat. New recruits report for 10 weeks of basic training at one of four boot camps across the United States. Training is broken down into three phases.

Red Phase

During the Red Phase, drill instructors focus on teaching teamwork. On the first day of boot camp, drill sergeants throw all new recruits' suitcases into a big pile. Recruits have to work quickly to find their own.

Recruits who stand out in any way will do a lot of push-ups until they learn to blend in. Drill sergeants want recruits to become a tight-knit group. Later in the Red Phase, recruits work together to hike through a dense forest using maps and compasses.

Recruits also learn how to handle firearms. Some recruits are given fake rifles known as "rubber ducks" until they learn how to handle real ones.

White Phase

During the White Phase, drill instructors work on building confidence. Recruits learn and practice shooting skills. They begin working with more complex weapons such as grenade launchers and machine guns. Soldiers must pass a shooting test by hitting at least 28 out of 40 pop-up targets.

An important part of boot camp is weapons training. Recruits learn to avoid "friendly-fire" accidents.

Blue Phase

In the Blue Phase, soldiers move into the field with their **platoon**. They train in day and nighttime combat and face **simulated** combat.

Drill sergeants get in the way and keep soldiers from being able to carry out their plans. For example, recruits eat a Meal, Ready-to-Eat (MRE) for breakfast, lunch, and dinner. It can take a new recruit about 15 minutes to figure out how to open and heat an MRE. But drill sergeants only give recruits 10 minutes to eat. Recruits learn quickly to solve this problem so they don't go hungry.

platoon—a U.S. military group made up of two to four squads of soldiers

simulated—pretend

Chapter 3

LIFE ON ACTIVE DUTY

An Army soldier can do many different types of jobs after completing basic training. These jobs are called military occupational specialites (MOS). Many soldiers go right into the infantry, while others learn different skills. There are many unusual jobs for soldiers, including broadcast specialists, artists, and even insect specialists called entomologists. They learn new skills at Advanced Individual Training (AIT).

Advanced Individual Training

Soldiers attend AIT right after boot camp. AIT is an extension of basic training. There are 17 AIT schools all over the country. There are several different programs at each AIT school. Soldiers can train for jobs working with tanks, jeeps, and airplanes. They can learn how to gather **intelligence** or how to work with **nuclear** energy. Depending on the job they are assigned, soldiers can attend AIT for a month to a year.

Broadcast Specialists

Soldiers who want to become journalists and television news broadcasters can learn the skills they will need at AIT training to become Army public affairs broadcast specialists. This AIT is 12 weeks long and teaches soldiers videography and video editing. They also learn voice skills for delivering news on television and on the radio.

Strong research and writing skills are needed for this MOS. Army public affairs broadcast specialists also train in public speaking and performing as a disc jockey.

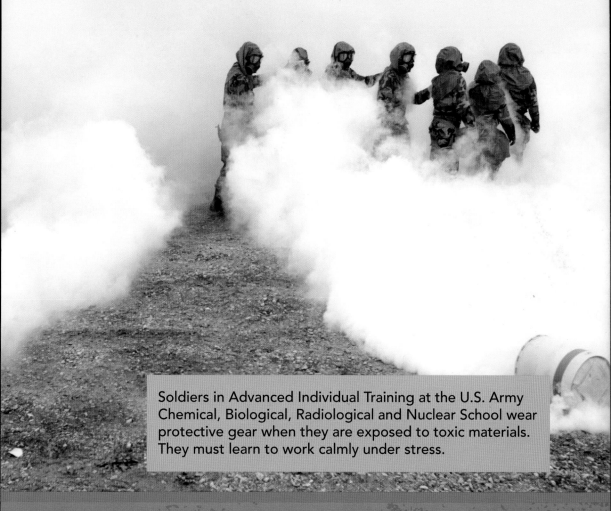

Soldiers in Advanced Individual Training at the U.S. Army Chemical, Biological, Radiological and Nuclear School wear protective gear when they are exposed to toxic materials. They must learn to work calmly under stress.

FACT Recruits train to use gas masks in a sealed room called "the gas chamber," where they are exposed for a short time to tear gas. Recruits must answer simple questions or say the alphabet correctly without their gas masks on or they are sent through the gas chamber again.

intelligence—secret information about an enemy's plans or actions

nuclear—energy converted by splitting two particles of matter called atoms

Army entomologists may be sent on humanitarian missions in rural parts of the world. If large animals become infected with disease-carrying insects, an army entomologist will help find a solution.

Entomologists

It isn't just tanks and bombs that soldiers have to worry about. Small pests cause problems too. Army entomologists study insects. They try to come up with ways to keep insects away from the soldiers to prevent the spread of diseases such as malaria. For example, entomologists might fill traps with a foul-smelling formula of rotted material to attract bugs. This gives soldiers relief from the bugs — but not from bad smells.

Multimedia Artists

Multimedia artists learn how to draw **freehand** and with the latest graphic arts technology. Their artwork is used to draw plans for battlefield strategies to share with commanders. Artists earn "secret" security clearance. This means that they are trusted with important combat information.

freehand—done without special tools or instruments

LIVING ON BASE

    Living on an Army base as a soldier is not the same as living at boot camp as a recruit. Recruits are not allowed to have any personal items at basic training, so they only need a small locker to keep their uniforms and equipment. Active-duty soldiers living on base will usually have their own room and more space for personal items.

Originally called Camp Bragg, Fort Bragg was founded in North Carolina in 1918.

Barracks

A soldier who decides to live off base will have to pay for housing. To keep costs low, many new soldiers choose to live on base. Sleeping spaces on base are like dormitories. Soldiers usually have their own room. Sometimes they share with a roommate.

Soldiers who live on base with their families are offered larger homes. These apartments or small houses have more bedrooms, closets, and larger living areas than dormitories for single soldiers. They also have small yards and are often near playgrounds and basketball courts for children to play. Pets larger than a goldfish are usually not allowed.

Chow Hall

The Army calls its cafeteria a chow hall. Soldiers who live in the barracks or dormitories on base eat in the chow hall for free. Chow halls usually serve at least four meals per day. Some serve meals around the clock.

Soldiers can bring their families to vacation spots such as the Hale Koa Hotel in Waikiki Beach, Hawaii, for a reduced cost. *Hale Koa* means "House of the Warrior."

HAVING FUN IN THE ARMY

A soldier's life can be stressful. The Army offers ways for soldiers to enjoy hobbies and recreation. The Army also offers opportunities for soldiers and their families to relax and enjoy downtime.

Armed Forces Recreation Centers

Armed Forces Recreation Centers are not fitness centers. They are fun places to go on vacation. Soldiers and their families can visit resorts in Hawaii and Florida. There are also several vacation spots in Europe and South Korea.

Hobbies

Some Army bases have hobby shops where soldiers and their families can learn how to create pottery, do woodworking, and even learn auto repair. The hobby shops sell the tools and equipment needed for these activities.

Chapter 4

SPECIAL FORCES

The Army Special Forces play a unique role in protecting the United States. They spend much of their time going on secret missions. When they fight, they fight with all they have. Special Forces are made up of soldiers "who have no quit in them." Army Special Forces units are based at Fort Bragg, North Carolina.

GREEN BERETS

There are about 5,500 active-duty Green Berets. It is their job to respond to combat and rescue missions all around the world. Most of what the Green Berets do is kept secret. Soldiers who want to train to become Green Berets must be able to do a minimum of 100 sit-ups in 2 minutes; do 100 push-ups in 2 minutes; and run 2 miles (3.2 km) in 12 to 14 minutes.

Green Beret candidates who make it to the Special Forces Assessment and Selection Course train from six months to a year, depending on the job they will do.

Guerilla Warfare

The Green Berets focus on guerilla warfare. They search for secret information about the enemy's plans and location. The Green Berets also lead raids and **ambushes**. Their goal is to stop enemy attacks, and to support and protect U.S. soldiers.

Army soldiers wear patrol caps with their combat uniforms — except for special operations soldiers such as the Green Berets, who have earned the right to wear special headgear called berets.

Warrior Diplomats

The Green Berets are trained to be **diplomats**. Diplomats influence others by using strong, persuasive speech and being sensitive to what others want and need. Green Berets can adapt easily to foreign customs. They might need to learn to eat certain foods or follow certain table manners to prepare for a mission in a different country. All Green Berets speak at least one foreign language.

ambush—a surprise attack

diplomat—a person who manages a country's affairs with other nations

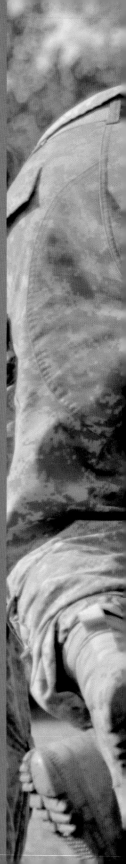

RANGERS

The Rangers are an **elite** Special Forces team. Training for a spot on the Rangers is difficult. There are three phases to Rangers training.

Benning Phase

Ranger candidates must crawl through the worm pit. The worm pit is a shallow, muddy pit. Candidates creep through on their backs and stomachs to avoid low-hanging barbed wire. Soldiers also make a 12-mile (19-km) hike without water, carrying 35 pounds (16 kilograms) of gear. Only 50 percent of Ranger students complete this phase.

Mountain Phase

Candidates spend weeks in rugged terrain. They are cold and tired most of the time. One of the toughest challenges is the log balance. They balance and walk on a log 35 feet (11 meters) in the air. Then they inch their way across a rope bridge, and finally drop into a pond. In another exercise, candidates must submerge in a pond and unload their heavy packs before they can rise to the surface.

Florida Phase

In this phase, Ranger candidates train in the water. They practice stream crossings and small boat movements in swamps and wetlands. They practice what it is like to go on a raid and patrol as guards.

FACT In August 2015, U.S. Army First Lieutenant Kirsten Griest and First Lieutenant Shaye Haver became the first women to ever graduate from U.S. Army Ranger school.

elite—the part or group having the highest quality or importance

When Ranger school opened to women in 2015, 19 women were accepted and three graduated. A few years earlier, the Pentagon ordered that all military positions, including combat roles, be open to women.

DELTA FORCE

Soldiers who join Delta Force keep what they do a secret. Delta Force is the most elite special operations force in the U.S. military.

All Delta Force recruits must be able to hit a target 600 yards (548 m) away with 100-percent accuracy.

Civilian Rescue

Though information about Delta Force is top secret, their training facility is believed to contain buses, trains, and even an airplane. They plan for different situations where civilian passengers could be held hostage. Delta Force's main goal is to make sure hostages are freed unhurt.

Unique Gear

Delta Force soldiers need special equipment. When they jump from extremely high altitudes — so high up that the oxygen is thin — they wear special helmets. These helmets provide oxygen so that soldiers can breathe.

Like other soldiers, Special Forces troops wear **infrared** goggles. These help soldiers see at night or in dark places. Some use inflatable, lightweight boats that move on both water and land. These are called amphibious vehicles. These special boats can even be used to launch from a helicopter.

On secret missions, the gear that Delta Force operatives wear, such as infrared goggles, helps them get the job done.

infrared—producing or using rays at the red end of the light spectrum

Chapter 5

DEPLOYMENT

When soldiers move overseas for a mission, it is called **deployment**. Army soldiers deploy more often and for longer periods of time than those who serve in other military branches.

Deployment Basics

The average deployment overseas is 12 months long. Sometimes soldiers will be kept longer than planned. The Army may keep soldiers longer to make sure operations are as safe and secure as possible. Sometimes friends and family at home will send care packages to soldiers who are deployed. Soldiers like to receive candy, gum, salty snacks, drink mixes, and items that can make MREs taste better, such as mustard and ketchup.

Who Gets Deployed?

The type of job a soldier has will decide how often he or she is deployed. Soldiers who are trained in combat will be sent to battle zones more often than personnel whose jobs don't involve fighting. However, soldiers who process forms and organize supplies are also needed to make sure deployments run smoothly.

  Pennies are not used on Army bases around the world because the Army considers them unnecessary and not worth the cost of shipping.

deployment—the movement of soldiers for military action

Deployed troops are separated from their families for a long time. Creating a sense of community while away from home is an important job that leaders in the Army take on.

Murphy's Law

Some soldiers believe in a superstition called "Murphy's Law." This is the belief that what can go wrong, will go wrong. Although this is supposed to be a joke, many soldiers agree that it can be all too real, especially in a battle zone.

Soldiers report one example of Murphy's Law: as soon as they jump in the shower, the alarm signaling incoming fire will sound, forcing them to run for cover. As soon as they try to sleep, noisy maintenance crews will get to work on vehicles and generators. Tired soldiers will have to listen to engines whirring all night.

Food in the Field

When hot food isn't available, soldiers eat MREs. A typical MRE will have a main meal, such as chili, spaghetti, or beef stew, and a side dish. They come with a flameless ration heater to heat the meal. MREs also come with a spoon, matches, creamer, sugar, salt, chewing gum, and toilet paper. Though they have enough nutrients and calories to keep soldiers healthy, many soldiers complain that they do not taste very good.

MREs used to be for soldiers only. Now they are available for civilians to buy for hiking or camping trips.

GLOSSARY

ambush (AM-bush)—a surprise attack

deployment (di-PLOY-ment)—the movement of soldiers for military action

diplomat (DIP-lo-mat)—a person who manages a country's affairs with other nations

elite (i-LEET)—the part or group having the highest quality or importance

enlist (in-LIST)—to voluntarily join a branch of the military

expel (ik-SPEL)—to throw out or ban

freehand (FREE-hand)—done without special tools or instruments

infrared (in-fruh-RED)—producing or using rays at the red end of the light spectrum

intelligence (in-TEL-uh-jenss)—secret information about an enemy's plans or actions

nuclear (NOO-klee-ur)—energy converted by splitting two particles of matter called atoms

platoon (pluh-TOON)—a U.S. military group made up of two to four squads of soldiers

recruit (ri-KROOT)—a person newly enlisted in the armed forces and not yet fully trained

simulated (SIM-yoo-LAY-ted)—pretend

varsity (VAR-si-tee)—the principal team representing a high school or college in a sport or other competition

READ MORE

Doeden, Matt. *Can You Survive in the Special Forces?: An Interactive Survival Adventure.* You Choose Books. Mankato, Minn.: Capstone Press, 2013.

Newman, Patricia. *Army Special Forces: Elite Operations.* Military Special Ops. Minneapolis: Lerner Publications Company, 2014.

Simons, Lisa M. B. *U.S. Army by the Numbers.* U.S. Military by the Numbers. Mankato, Minn.: Capstone Press, 2014.

INTERNET SITES

Use FactHound to find Internet sites related to this book:

Visit *www.facthound.com*

Just type in 9781515774297 and go.

Super-cool stuff!

Check out projects, games and lots more at
www.capstonekids.com

INDEX